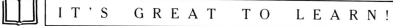

IT'S GREAT TO LEARN!

John Burningham's
abc

CROWN PUBLISHERS, INC.   NEW YORK

Aa

alligator

Bb

bear

Cc

cow

Dd

duck

Ee

elephant

Ff

flowers

G g

goat

Hh

hippopotamus

I i

ice cream

J j juggler

K k

kangaroo

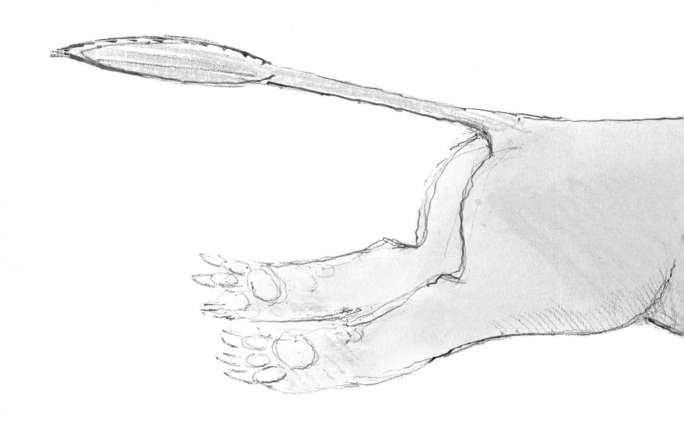

L l

lion

Mm

monkey

Nn

newt

Oo

ostrich

P p

parrot

Qq

queen

Rr

rabbit

Ss

snake

Tt

turtle

Uu

umbrella

V v

violin

W w

wasp

Xx

xylophone

Yy

yak

Z z

zebra